THE 10 S TO SUCCEED IN SPORTS OR BUSINESS

JOSH CEPE

WWW.10S.LIFE

THE 10 S TO SUCCEED IN SPORTS OR BUSINESS

Copyright © 2018 JOSH CEPE

All rights reserved.

ISBN: **9781731179852**

WWW.10S.LIFE

THE 10 S TO SUCCEED IN SPORTS OR BUSINESS

THIS BOOK CONTAINS
THE SECRET
INGREDIENTS OF
SUCCESS
FOR HUNGRY SPORTS
PLAYER AND
ENTREPRENEURS

WWW.10S.LIFE

WARNING: You are about to discover lots of things that you will only find in this book.

THE 10 S TO SUCCEED IN SPORTS OR BUSINESS

CONTENTS

	Acknowledgments	VI
	Introduction	VII
	The Author	VIII
	Objective	10
	SLAP Technique	14
	LICK ASS Technique	15
	CEPE System	16
	CEPE Attitudes	20
	The Objective Of A Business	37
	The Objective Of A Sport Player	44
	Top 10 Most Successful Sportsmen Of All Time	50
	Top 10 Most Inspiring Entrepreneurs Around The Globe	57
	Top 10 Successful Entrepreneurs Around The World	68
	Top 10 Successful Products	79
1	Chapter - Strength	88
2	Chapter - Speed	93
3	Chapter - Stamina	98
4	Chapter - Strategy	103
5	Chapter - Skills	108
6	Chapter - Spirit	113
7	Chapter – Self-Confidence	117
8	Chapter – Self-Control	122
9	Chapter – Self-Discipline	126
10	Chapter – Self-improvement	130
	Top 10 Success Books	134

WWW.10S.LIFE

ACKNOWLEDGMENTS

I would like to say THANK YOU! to all the people who helped me writing this book specially YOU! I wish you all the best and I hope you enjoy reading this. Have a great day!

INTRODUCTION

CONGRATULATIONS!
YOU AREABOUT TO DISCOVER THE 10 S TO SUCEED IN SPORTS OR BUSINESS.

"THERE ARE 3 GROUPS OF PEOPLE IN THIS WORLD. THE FIRST GROUP OF PEOPLE WHO MOST OF THE TIME TALKING ABOUT OTHER PEOPLE. THE SECOND GROUP OF PEOPLE WHO TALK ABOUT DIFFERENT PLACES THEY HAVE BEEN TO. THE THIRD GROUP OF PEOPLE WHO MOST OF THE TIME TALKING ABOUT IDEAS, CONCEPTS, AND BUSINESS." - UNKNOWN

IT DOESN'T MATTER WHICH GROUP YOU ARE IN. IF YOU ARE READING THIS BOOK OR EBOOK, THEN THIS IS FOR YOU.

THE AUTHOR

This book or eBook is not about the author. This is about the third group of people, what makes them different from other 2 groups and what makes them successful as an entrepreneur or as a business owner. When I've been thinking about the ingredients of success I realized they all start with "S" and I also realized that both sports and business have the same ingredients of success. When I went to Google and search for the 10 ingredients of success in Sports or Business, I couldn't find the exact information I'm looking for so for me this is a big opportunity. I asked myself "What if there are many people also searching for the same thing I'm searching for?". Since "Speed" is one of the 10 "S", I didn't want to miss the opportunity to even it was late at night, I turned my computer on and made a to-do-list to make this happen.

This may not be over 200 pages, but the information you are about to learn is equivalent to 10 books. It's always better to read a few pages with all the information you need in it than reading a book with more than two hundred pages full of things you don't need.

THE 10 S TO SUCCEED IN SPORTS OR BUSINESS

OBJECTIVE

The author's objective for writing this book is to publish this book as soon as possible to meet the deadline of the author's goal. It's not author's objective to make this book or any part
of this book to be perfect. It is expected that you as a reader will notice or find some parts in this book that may be inappropriate or just
doesn't make sense. That's why it's author's objective to encourage all readers to suggest an edit or improvements, recommend a better contents and become one of the editors or contributors of
this book called THE 10 S TO SUCCED IN SPORTS OR BUSINESS. Please tell us what you think by sending us an email at ideas@10s.life and if your ideas has been chosen, it will be added
to the updated version of this book and your name and other details as well as the location of the contents will be added below and other pages.

Editor/Contributor
Name:
Business/company:
Website:
Contents:
Pages:

Editor/Contributor
Name:
Business/company:
Website:
Contents:
Pages:
_____

Editor/Contributor
Name:
Business/company:
Website:
Contents:
Pages:
_____

Editor/Contributor
Name:
Business/company:
Website:
Contents:
Pages:
_____

Editor/Contributor
Name:
Business/company:
Website:
Contents:
Pages:

Editor/Contributor
Name:
Business/company:
Website:
Contents:
Pages:

Editor/Contributor
Name:
Business/company:
Website:
Contents:
Pages:

Editor/Contributor
Name:
Business/company:
Website:
Contents:
Pages:

Editor/Contributor
Name:
Business/company:
Website:
Contents:
Pages:

Editor/Contributor
Name:
Business/company:
Website:
Contents:
Pages:

SLAP TECHNIQUE

S - Show people how it's done properly and correctly.

L - Let them do it.

A - Assess them if they are doing the task properly and correctly.

P - Plan their next task and make sure they learn something new every day.

LICK ASS TECHNIQUE

Now that you know how to SLAP people, do you know that the best and fastest way to learn anything is by learning how to LICK ASS? Let me show you how. In order to learn better and faster, you need to..

L -Listen carefully to your teacher, instructor or trainer.
I -Inform your teacher, instructor or trainer if something is unclear.
C -Clarify things to make sure you understand the instruction correctly.
K -Keep doing the 1st 3 steps and Keep up the good work! If there is any doubt, make sure you...
A -Ask questions or Ask for help if needed.
S -Speak with other students or trainees and...
S -Share knowledge and experience. Because there are things that others know but you don't. And there are things you know but others don't know.

CEPE SYSTEM

If you are thinking about starting a part time or full time business or you are just looking for a better system to get things done properly
and correctly and minimize the risk of losing heaps of money and
time, then this system will be your hero.

    C -Customers, Contents, Competition
    E -Equipment or tooling, Education, Employee
    P -Products, Process or Procedure
    E -End goal

It's very important in business that you know the 3 C's and you know how to use it to save time and money and to give you more sales.

Customers - Having the right customers or audience will surely save you lots of money and time on advertising. For example, if your business is selling beauty products, you need to make sure your target customers are people who are more likely to buy your products. In this case, women are mostly your buying customer.

You also need to make sure that if you are going to spend money on advertising, you need to know which group of women can afford to buy your product. You also need to consider their age and nationality. It's a waste of time and money showing or selling your product to people who doesn't need it or can't afford it.

Contents - Before registering a business and domain name for website, spending money to get a good looking website and buying expensive equipment, you need to make sure you are able to produce all the contents you need. Because if you don't, it means you have chosen the wrong product or services.

Doing something you know is different from doing something you love. If you have chosen something you really love to do, you will always be able to produce the right contents for your website and you will never lose interest to anything you do.

Competition - It's very important that you have an idea about your competition. If you are just starting your business, you don't want to compete with bigger brand or company who already gained trusts from millions of people. Unless your product is really unique, it's better to choose something that people needs or wants but not available or very limited in your area.

Let's talk about how the 3 E's can save you time and money.

Equipment - Having the right equipment or tooling will definitely save you time and money. Many people would buy cheap computer, software, electronic gadgets but then realized they don't have all the things they need or it started to play up since it's low quality products.

A rich man said, if you want to become rich you need to buy expensive items with very high quality. Because when you buy high quality products, it will last long.

When a product has low quality, it will not last long. It means you will need to buy a new one very soon since you need it. Make sure you always purchase the high quality equipment, software or tools so that you don't end up losing money buying the same thing again and again.

Education - In business, having a degree is a bonus but having the right education or knowledge is very important. For example, you need a beautiful website done for your business but you don't have a good idea of how much you should be spending. Many website company or developer would ask business owner if they have experience on having a website done in the past. Because that would give them an idea if they will charge you more for a website.

If you don't know all the things you need to have in your website, you will end up paying for additional works since you will realize that your website actually needs more than just a good design, high quality images and beautiful logo.

Employee - Hiring an employee or team to help you with your business is not enough but choosing the right employee is. Having the right team in your business means you are achieving each business goals since they know what they are doing and they know why they are doing it.

CEPE ATTITUDES

To better help you choose the right employee for your business, it's important that you know why people do some things but don't like doing other things.

Cooperative Attitude - This is our attitude when even we don't know a particular task, we are willing to do it especially if an instruction or procedure is available or someone will show you how to do it.

Eclectic Attitude - This is our attitude when we don't like doing a particular task even we have done it before and we know how to do it. People with eclectic attitude always choose the best. It's ok to be choosy sometimes at work as long as it's not all the time. It's acceptable to say no to a job or task if you feel unsafe or you know you are not authorized to perform it or you are just feeling sick.

Player Attitude - This is our attitude when we like doing a particular task since we know how to do it and we are good doing it. Think about all the sports players whether it's basketball, football, tennis, soccer, golf, boxing and other sports, each of them has been chosen to play because they know how to play, they are good at it and they like what they do.

End Attitude - This is our attitude when we say no to a job or task since we haven't done it before or the task is just something we are not interested in. It's acceptable if the task needs authorization or license to do it.

Let's talk about the 3 P's for your business.
Product - Choosing the right product is one of the most important in business. Good product research is a must. You need to think about how many people would buy your product and how much would you earn in a monthly basis. You need to make sure your monthly sales profit is higher than your monthly expenses to run your business.

Process - According to Wikipedia, a process is a set of activities that interact to produce a result. Having a good process, procedure or system in your business will surely save you lots of time and money doing the same thing over and over again. For example, instead of teaching or explaining things or rules to a new employee, you make a video or written instruction that anyone can read and understand.

You need to accept that every part of your team will not stay forever and for some reason will quit. If this happens, your good process or system will prevent you from starting from the beginning. Any experience and knowledge shared by your team needs to be added to your process or system.

A process or system doesn't need to be perfect. In fact, it will never be perfect as new technology is introduced and new rules needs to be followed. You can only improve your process, procedure or system.

Plan - Business owners and entrepreneurs have three types of plan that normally have to dealt with.

Business Plan
What are your business plan? Do you have any plan to have a branch in other places? Do you plan to start a new business once everything is running smoothly and someone is running it for you?

Personal Plan
What are your personal plan? If you are single, are you planning to get married soon? Do you have any plans to travel? Are you planning to study to have the right education for your business? Whatever your plan is, make sure it's not going to affect the time you need to spend in your business. If you are just starting in business, it's not a good idea to get married then have a baby as you need to divide all

your time for your family, business, work if you still have full time job and for yourself. Make sure you still have enough time to rest and enjoy.

Family Plan
If you have your own family already, you need to understand that you will get to the point that you need to choose between your business and family.

There will be times that you will have a very important business meetings as well as your partner special day or kids graduation day at the same time. We normally see this situation on TV or movies but this happens in real life.

Planning everything properly will prevent you from losing business opportunities and important things in your life.

End Goal

Knowing your end goal is very important in business. Remember, if you don't know what you are looking for, you will never find it. You are not in business just to have enough money to pay the bills. You are in business because you want to have financial freedom. You want to be able to provide anything that your family needs. You want to be able to travel around the world without any worries. Perhaps you want to be able to help other people by providing them jobs, money, food, shelter, clean water and many things.

Write down your end goal below by filling in the blanks. (Please use pencil with eraser as you might get a better idea later on.)

On_____
I,
will_____
_____
_____.

End Goal is achieved by completing each big tasks. Each Big Task consists of 2 or more small tasks.

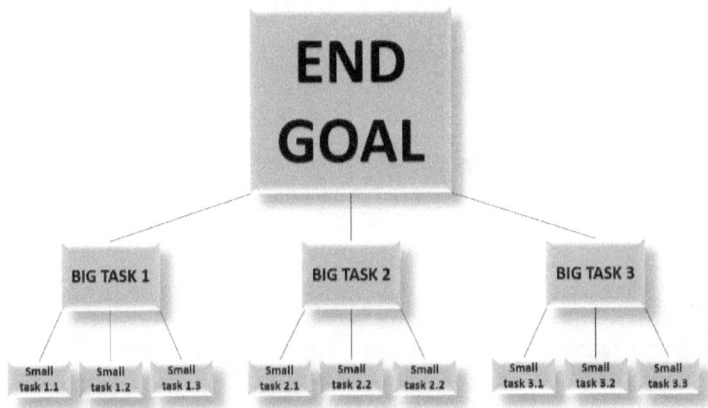

Write down your end goal on top of the box below. Then, make a lists of the things that you need to do in order to reach your end goal. Decide when you want or need it done. Then tick the status box when it's done. You will need to come back on this page every time each Big task is completed. If you have more than 10 Big Task, feel free to add more below.

END GOAL: _____

BIG TASKS	Date	Status
1.		
2.		
3.		
4.		
5.		
6.		
7.		
8.		
9.		
10.		

Now write down each big task description on top of the box below. Then, make a lists of the things that you need to do in order to complete it. Decide when you want or need each small task done. Then tick the status box when done.

BIG TASK DESCRIPTION: _____

small tasks	Date	Status
1.		
2.		
3.		
4.		
5.		
6.		
7.		
8.		
9.		
10.		

Once all small tasks are done, go back to your lists of Big Task and tick the status box.

Now write down your next big task description on top of the box below. Then, make a lists of the things that you need to do in order to complete it. Decide when you want or need each small task done. Then tick the status box when done.

BIG TASK DESCRIPTION: _____

small tasks	Date	Status
1.		
2.		
3.		
4.		
5.		
6.		
7.		
8.		
9.		
10.		

Once all small tasks are done, go back to your lists of Big Task and tick the status box.

Now write down your next big task description on top of the box below. Then, make a lists of the things that you need to do in order to complete it. Decide when you want or need each small task done. Then tick the status box when done.

BIG TASK DESCRIPTION: _____

small tasks	Date	Status
1.		
2.		
3.		
4.		
5.		
6.		
7.		
8.		
9.		
10.		

Once all small tasks are done, go back to your lists of Big Task and tick the status box.

Now write down your next big task description on top of the box below. Then, make a lists of the things that you need to do in order to complete it. Decide when you want or need each small task done. Then tick the status box when done.

BIG TASK DESCRIPTION: _____

small tasks	Date	Status
1.		
2.		
3.		
4.		
5.		
6.		
7.		
8.		
9.		
10.		

Once all small tasks are done, go back to your lists of Big Task and tick the status box.

Now write down your next big task description on top of the box below. Then, make a lists of the things that you need to do in order to complete it. Decide when you want or need each small task done. Then tick the status box when done.

BIG TASK DESCRIPTION: _____

small tasks	Date	Status
1.		
2.		
3.		
4.		
5.		
6.		
7.		
8.		
9.		
10.		

Once all small tasks are done, go back to your lists of Big Task and tick the status box.

Now write down your next big task description on top of the box below. Then, make a lists of the things that you need to do in order to complete it. Decide when you want or need each small task done. Then tick the status box when done.

BIG TASK DESCRIPTION: _____

small tasks	Date	Status
1.		
2.		
3.		
4.		
5.		
6.		
7.		
8.		
9.		
10.		

Once all small tasks are done, go back to your lists of Big Task and tick the status box.

Now write down your next big task description on top of the box below. Then, make a lists of the things that you need to do in order to complete it. Decide when you want or need each small task done. Then tick the status box when done.

BIG TASK DESCRIPTION: _____

small tasks	Date	Status
1.		
2.		
3.		
4.		
5.		
6.		
7.		
8.		
9.		
10.		

Once all small tasks are done, go back to your lists of Big Task and tick the status box.

Now write down your next big task description on top of the box below. Then, make a lists of the things that you need to do in order to complete it. Decide when you want or need each small task done. Then tick the status box when done.

BIG TASK DESCRIPTION: _____

small tasks	Date	Status
1.		
2.		
3.		
4.		
5.		
6.		
7.		
8.		
9.		
10.		

Once all small tasks are done, go back to your lists of Big Task and tick the status box.

Now write down your next big task description on top of the box below. Then, make a lists of the things that you need to do in order to complete it. Decide when you want or need each small task done. Then tick the status box when done.

BIG TASK DESCRIPTION: _____

small tasks	Date	Status
1.		
2.		
3.		
4.		
5.		
6.		
7.		
8.		
9.		
10.		

Once all small tasks are done, go back to your lists of Big Task and tick the status box.

Now write down your next big task description on top of the box below. Then, make a lists of the things that you need to do in order to complete it. Decide when you want or need each small task done. Then tick the status box when done.

BIG TASK DESCRIPTION: _____

small tasks	Date	Status
1.		
2.		
3.		
4.		
5.		
6.		
7.		
8.		
9.		
10.		

Once all small tasks are done, go back to your lists of Big Task and tick the status box.

The Objective of a Business

Business objectives represent the purpose for which that business has been started. Objectives do govern and guide both the behavior and actions of a business entity. Your objectives also entail the results you intend to attain and maintain when you operate and expand your business.

Though the first objective for most businesses is to make profit, they should outline other objectives. For one, the business should lay out strategies on how to acquire customers. Most importantly, you should know how to retain those customers and make them come back for more products/services.

Second, you should outline your objective on how to sell your services or products to those customers. Another objective is to get paid by your customers and clients.

When an entrepreneur realizes a problem, they aim at starting a business just to provide a solution to that problem. Most essentially, is to come up with a product/service that people need almost every day. In doing so, for sure, you'll always make lots of sales.

SMART business objectives

An objective provides a business an openly defined target. The owner can then make plans to attain these targets. It is in doing so that employees get motivated. As a dedicated entrepreneur, for sure, you'll be concerned with each aspect of your company.

Hence, you must set out clear and SMART goals for your business. But what do SMART objectives mean?

"S" means Specific: the objectives should aim at what your business does. As in the objective should be specific to your business.

"M" stands for Measurable: your objective should have a value over a certain period. For instance, you aim at selling

goods/services worth $10,000 in the next 6 months.

"A" stands for Agreed: the objective should be agreed upon by everyone trying to attain it.

"R" stands for Realistic: your objectives should be challenging. However, you should be able to achieve them using the resources that you already have.

"T" stands for Time Specific: objectives should have a time limit – like by year end you want to have acquired 10,000 customers.

Setting out an all-inclusive list of objectives is a great foundation for your business's planning.

3 Major Objectives of a Business
1. Acquire customers
Setting out objectives on how to acquire new customers is challenging. However, with the use of some tactics and strategies, you can get customers. Without a solid strategy, your business will seriously have a difficult time trying to grow in any meaningful way.

That said, the most challenging part of scaling a business is selecting the right channel for attracting new customers.

One of the strategies you can use is unopened emails to boost engagement. The objective here is to attract more people into reading the emails and engaging. However, be careful when sending emails. You should target only the subscribers that haven't opened your emails.

Republishing and updating old content is another strategy to get customers. This strategy aims at generating more search traffic to your existing content on your blog. To attain this objective, you should identify those pages on your site that provide lots of organic search traffic. Top-of-the-funnel content such as blog articles attracts traffic.

Equally important, you can acquire new customers by integrating your existing products with others. As a result, you'll provide enhanced user experience. You can get new customers by increasing organic search traffic by ranking for all the keywords related to the location and industries you target.

2. Sell products or services

After getting customers, the other objective is to sell your products or services. For customers to buy from you, you must offer them good experience, ensure they feel treated fairly and boost customer retention.

Keeping your customers satisfied has everything to do with offering high-quality products/services. So, your staff should always respond to grievances from customers. The major aim here is to resolve customer's complaint to their satisfaction.

Moreover, you should ensure that you meet the needs for every customer. As different as customers are, everyone deserves respect. Therefore, make sure you instruct your employees to act like professionals every time a customer walks into your store. Besides acquiring customers and ensuring they buy your products, you should boost repeat business. Improving customer retention and getting repeat business is an objective that should never miss on your list.

3. Get paid

Profit maximization is another objective of a business. But for a business to be profitable they must sell products and customers must pay. You should offer customers flexible modes of payments. These payment methods should suit both direct customers and Business-to-Business.

Options include cash, check, credit cards, and online payments. Each option suits specific business where some businesses use more than one. Likewise, each payment option has pros and cons. Checks are risky and outdated; though many businesses accept them. A small business might not be able to verify whether a check is good or whether the owner's account has enough funds.

Cash, on the other hand, seems as the best option. However, businesses accepting cash do so for some reasons. Some do so to report low tax value. Others accept cash because they can hardly afford the merchant fees associated with the processing of debit and credit cards.

Credit card is another payment method that most businesses use across the globe. This option, however, usually has its own cost. Incidental fees, flat fees, and transnational fees are some of those costs.

Online payment is another option to get paid. It comes with security and convenience issues. Just as other payment methods, online payments have their benefits and drawbacks. For instance, an online payment provides a reliable, faster and cheaper way to get paid. Ensure you evaluate each to see which one suits your business and customers.

The bottom line
Setting out smart objectives is important for every business to succeed. However, those objectives may change with time due to certain reasons. A business may attain one objective and want to proceed onto the next one. For instance, when a business survives in the first year, it may proceed to boosting profit in the next year.

Besides attaining one objective, a business can change its objectives whenever the competitive environment changes. When a competitor launches new products then your business should change its objectives. Further, technology keeps on changing with new designs coming up. Therefore, a business should change its production and sales targets.

Nonetheless, one major objective of a business is to provide solutions to problems that people are facing. In doing so, the business will acquire new customers or clients and get regular repurchases

The Objectives Of a Sport Player

Players go through a hard time to define success. Most coaches and athletes also define success in terms of wins, results, rankings or times. Even though results determine the success of players, preoccupation with them may affect your chances of achieving your goals, and you might produce feelings of frustrations and disappointments. By focusing on results, you will not achieve anything before the sports competition starts. Moreover, you will get nervous even before the competition starts, and you might miss a chance to participate.

When planning to enter a new season, your dream might be to lift the league trophy at the end of that season. Some other people might have a goal of avoiding relegation and taking the prize of their rivals within the process. But regardless of your goals, it is important you start every season by setting your main objective. By having an objective, you will enjoy many benefits. Here are the objectives to keep in mind.

Get a chance to play
Before the game, you will not have the ability to control the games. Actually, the only thing you can

control is your preparation. Therefore, you should work out well so that when the game starts you will be able to say that you are adequately prepared to achieve your goals or those of your team.

Adequate preparation will help you get a chance to play. If you happen to enter in a field without any preparations, you will have a zero chance of winning because your competitors might be better than you or adequately prepared. Proper preparation does not mean that you will have a 100 percent chance of success – but your winning chances will be better.

If you are not adequately prepared to do your best in the field, you are unlikely to get a chance of playing. The purpose of preparations is to help you get the chance. Every team manager would want to have players who can perform well and score more goals.

To prepare for sports, you should look at everything that is within your control, particularly the things that can affect your performance, and take another step towards maximizing the areas.

Some of the things that can affect your performance in sport include equipment, nutrition, sleep, and pre-game warm-ups. When preparing for a game, you should ensure that you have the necessary equipment – such as sports gear – and you are physically prepared. You will, therefore, need to warm-up, breathe and reach your intensity. Mental preparation is also important and it involves mindset, focus, and imagery.

So, when working to get a chance to play, you will feel adequately prepared and confident to offer great results.

Make a score
After getting a chance to play, you will have to work to get the results you desire. If you have already set your outcome goals, then you should work to achieve them in all matches. In other words, you will have to push your limits and compete with abandonment.

The goal is seemingly obvious to most individuals because they believe that holding back will never work. Nothing should prevent you from working to achieve the goal each time you compete. However, with this goal in your mind, you will also be putting yourself at a higher risk of the involved dangers and you might not achieve anything. You might also make costly mistakes when in the field.

In other words, the goal might lead to failure – the worst thing to experience. That is what each player should work to prevent. You are likely to fail if the goal remains in your mind throughout. Wait for opportunities to present themselves and use them.

To win the game
When in a competition, the goal of most players is usually to make a solid performance. Perhaps, you have witnessed a string of bad performances for a long time, and now you want to win a game to break it without making any major mistakes. With that in mind, you will perform cautiously. After the competition has ended, you will feel relieved about not having a major fail.

But, what are the results of the attitudes? Mostly, the result is usually an average performance or a loss. Your immediate reaction might be regret. You will wish that you had played differently. Differently put, you will start blaming yourself for not risking mistakes instead of performing tentatively. You will also begin looking back at the competition and wishing you had burdened yourself instead of holding back.

Regret is a good value in sports and personal life. Anyone would want fewer regrets. After a game, season or career, you should confidently say, "I did my best". You might have missed attaining your greatest goal, but you played humanely enough to achieve what you got.

Actually, you will be disappointed for not achieving the goal, but you will get over the feeling. You will also get pride and inspiration after realizing that you worked hard to achieve the goal.

The goal setting process
In your goal planning, you have to visualize and prepare adequately. Because Olympians are always disciplined and focused, they are able to write out their visualization plan, when to do it, how to do it, the practice and the implementation.

With a good plan, they are able to report great short and long-term results. Researchers and sports experts have ways of setting sports goals to ensure success.

They have also developed a great acronym to help players set their goals: SMART. Each goal you set should be Specific, Measurable, Attainable, Relevant and Time Specific. With that in mind, you should be able to write the goals down, determine the measurement for your goals, set the time limit, identify the main obstacles and overcome them. You should also be able to review the goals and monitor your progress.

Conclusion

To achieve your main goals in sports, you have to use every available opportunity. But when you fail to achieve the goals, you are unlikely to get the results you desire in life. Success is not always guaranteed – no matter how hard you try. However, by committing to and consistently working towards the goals, you will achieve something.

Top 10 Most Successful Sportsmen of All Time

Getting up and engaging in a physical activity is always beneficial for you. Whether you may be doing it for a health benefit or for fun. However, you may need to be aware of what you are getting yourself involved.

There are some activities that may have few to no rules and have more than one way to execute. These are mostly games. On the other hand, Sports involves a series of intense activities in a certain procedure with very specific rules and can be very competitive.

As the years have gone by, various types of Sports have continued to emerge and become popular among us; both locally and internationally. And even as a particular Sport engages many, certain players seem to thrive in representing their respective Sports from all over the world making it even more thrilling and exciting.

Here are some of our Sports heroes who have represented the world marvelously in the journey:

Serena Williams - Tennis
Serena Williams went pro in 1995 and ever since she owned the sport. It has been twenty years and she is still the most dominant athlete in both male and female participants of any of the sports in existence. Besides having four Olympic gold medals, 23 Grand Slam title and being a major Open era champion, Serena's sheer talent and incredible sports appeal have impacted the world of tennis in a great way.

Roger Federer - Tennis
Since 2002, Federer has continued to play tennis at a high level hence being ranked top 10. His list of records is endless and among them are; 17 Grand Slam singles titles, reaching each Grand Slam at least 5 times as well as holding position 1 for 302weeks. Federer is still regarded as the world's best tennis player as he is among the Golden era of men's tennis.

Michael Schumacher - F1

In addition to all the thrill and speed in the Grand Prix, there is great talent and expertise in the one and only Michael Schumacher. He has an incredible track record and is the best Formula 1 driver the world has come to know in his vibrant 15year career. Mr. Schumacher proved himself by winning 91 Grand Prix races and accumulate 7 World Championships hence establishing him as the best driver there is.

Additionally, between the years 2000- 2004, he had attained 5 titles consecutively. This guy loved the sport enough to resurface 4 years after retiring. His second appearance was not as successful as the first with only one podium finish in a span of three years. Besides, his dimmed light in the second phase, his dominance had already made its mark in Formula 1 driving.

Michael Phelps - Swimming

To be a good swimmer a lot of work must be put in. Michael Phelps mastered the art and garnered himself 18 gold medals in a span of 3 Olympic Games. Due to this, Phelps automatically became the most successful athlete in all the three Olympics that he had participated and had won.

His physique played a major role in his success too; with a wingspan that was 4 inches more than his height at 80 inches, there was no defeating him at all. Phelps made up his mind and announced his desire to retire in 2014.

Usain Bolt - Runner

Putting one foot in front of the other does not seem like such a hard task, but how fast can you do it? Can you cover 100m in 10 seconds? Well, Usain Bolt would not cover 100 m in 10 seconds but instead would finish it in 9.58 seconds almost without breaking a single sweat.

During the 2009 Olympic Games in Beijing, Usain Bolt seemed to have his runs figured out before he even got to the competing venue. All he did while in Beijing as he prepared for his race was eat some chicken nuggets and sleep and with just that managed to set new records in almost all his races that year.

From the 100 m to the 200 m and even to the 4 x 100 meters relay. He didn't finish there. In the nest Olympic being held in London, Usain won gold medals in all three while setting a new record to the 4 x 100 meter relay.

Throughout his career as an athlete, Usain Bolt has smashed unimaginable records.

Michael Jordan - Basketball

Whenever basketball is mentioned, the first name that comes to mind is Michael Jordan. Ever wondered why he is such a household name? Well, in the 90s, Jordan brought the thrill to any basketball game he was playing. He managed to attain the NBA championship 6 times and Most Valuable player 5 times alongside other titles to his name.

Finally, in 1999, ESPN named him as the greatest champion of the entire 20th century. He made basketball a household name beyond the boundaries of the USA.

Muhammad Ali - Boxing

For those born in the early 90s, you must agree that Muhammad Ali is a legend. He has been known as the greatest sportsman of all time due to his resilience and consistency that is driven by his passion to win his fights.

He took part in the greatest fights known such as;

The Fight of The Century, Thrilla in Manila as well as The Rumble in the Jungle. Despite his wonderful performance, Ali was stripped of his title for refusing to fight in the Vietnam War. Additionally, he had some inspiring quotes to add.

Pele - Soccer

Pele is the all-time top scorer in the world most popular sport; soccer. He is a record three-time World Cup winner and is also the top scorer in history. He started off in the Brazilian national team and with time managed to accomplish 1283 goals in the 1363 games played. Most of his career was for a team known as Santos before finishing off at the New York Cosmos. This great man helped put America on the map when it comes to soccer.

Ric Flair - Wrestling

Ric Flair is a 16-time world heavyweight champion who assisted in discovering talent by exploring various territories in the country and challenging the best he could find. He set a high standard for how wrestlers should speak, dress and carry themselves, in general, making him a demi-god among men. He had great influence in the world of wrestling that can still be felt.

Jackie Joyner-Kersee - Long Jump

Joyner-Kersee was voted Sports Illustrator for Women's Greatest Female Athlete of the 20th century when she won gold in the heptathlon and long jump during the Olympic Games in Seoul in 1988.

In 1992, she retained her position in the heptathlon as well as the best top 6 results ever achieved to date. She achieved this despite her severe Asthmatic condition.

No matter the sports one chooses to do, it must be done to the best in order to make it popular to the world around. A lot of commitment goes into good training to get well-deserved recognition and make it count as Muhammad Ali said; "I'm not the greatest; I'm the double greatest. Not only do I knock ?em out, but I also pick the round"

Top 10 Most Inspiring Entrepreneurs Around The Globe

It is a fact that everybody dreams of making it big in life, want to leave their cubicles behind, bid goodbye to their nagging boss, get away from the unhealthy corporate culture and control their own destiny, become their own boss. Though everyone wants all this, a very achieve it. This perhaps is partly because people think they can make it big only if they have great qualifications or a huge amount of money to invest. However, this is not true, there are many entrepreneurs who are immensely successful and it is only and only because they dared to dream and put in all their efforts into making that dream become a reality.

Without wasting a moment let us get to learn about such top 10 successful entrepreneurs and their journey that is sure to be inspiring for one and all.

1. Jan Koum
Born in the Soviet Union, Jan Koum moved to California in 1992 with his grandmother and mother and started living in a small apartment that they were lucky to receive because of a social support program that was started by the state.

When he was 16, Koum, in order to support his mother took up a cleaning job in some grocery store. After he learned how to code he became Yahoo's infrastructure engineer and worked there for 9 years.

All this was good, but the life-changing moment for Koum came in the year 2009 when he understood the potential of Apple's app store. Just a week later he created WhatsApp that would offer push notifications and thus the app would serve as an alternative to the normal text messaging. As Facebook acquired WhatsApp for $19bn and Koum earned a position as one of its board of directors, it attracted Mark Zuckerberg's attention as well. In April 2018, Jan Koum stepped down from this position yet it is said he already had made more than $9 billion.

2. J.K. Rowling

J.K. Rowling is one such name that hardly anyone has not heard of or not been a fan. Her book Harry Potter has become a household name with kids and adults being equal fans. She certainly is popular and minting money now but this was not always the case. Before she introduced to the world her imaginary world of wizards and witches, J.K.

Rowling was struggling as a single mother and living on welfare. As they say ?pen is mightier than the sword' her ability to pen down her imagination has today resulted in her having a net worth of a whopping $1 million. People have such strange things to say about her like she had sold her soul to the demons/devils in return for her inspiration to write Harry Potter, but then that is how people react when they see someone become so big from being just one like them. This, however, does show that if you have a talent, even if it is writing, do not underestimate it.

3. Hans Christian Anderson

The self-starter attitude and great determination of Hans Christian Anderson make him find a place in this list of the top 10 most successful entrepreneurs. Anderson's financial condition as a child was not good, but at the tender age of 14 he went off to Copenhagen all alone when he was told by a fortuneteller that even though during his early years he would suffer, gradually he would succeed and become popular.

These predictions indeed came true as Anderson tried his luck in acting and singing but failed completely. Luckily, the Royal Danish Theater's director saw a spark in Anderson because of which he took him under his care and sponsored his education. He used to be terribly teased when in school and students and even the headmaster used to harass him badly. These certainly were the darkest period of his life as he himself claims.

After he left school, Anderson started publishing his writings and his fairy tales started getting very popular and as the fortuneteller promised he started earning great fame. What he had faced as a child always stayed with him and drawing inspiration from how his mother would have had to beg on the streets when she was a young girl he wrote The Little Match Girl. Hans Christian Anderson is popular even today for his beautiful fairy tales, and many of these have even been inspirations for Disney animation classics.

4. Richard Branson

This list of the top 10 successful entrepreneurs cannot be complete without mentioning Richard Branson who pretty successfully has tried his hand at many lines of investment in the last 40 years. This certainly might not have been expected from someone who was not good at school and was later diagnosed with dyslexia.

He also got the title of Virgin on his very first enterprise, which certainly was not a good title. However, his very first venture was an immensely profitable reselling and importing of music records (during the 1960s), and at the same time he even managed the famous Student magazine, and because of this, he could open his own dedicated record store in 1971 in London. The profits that he made from this venture were used to set up Virgin records, in which he worked with many artists that he had earlier interviewed for the Student magazine.

Branson has also made and developed market leading services and products in media, rail transport, aviation, beverages, and so on. His net worth is about $4.9bn as he keeps on investing the profits he makes from one venture into developing yet another.

5. Steve Jobs
Yet another name in this list that surely everyone knows about, Steve Jobs was not always lucky, not always moneyed, and in fact, had to drop out of college as his family did not have enough money to support his education. Unofficially he continued to attend classes, went to Hare Krishna temple to get free meals, and would return Coke bottles for change. The calligraphy class that Jobs attended helped him create the font design and typefaces for Mac. However, he never stopped putting in efforts and this paved the way for an amazing career and then he ended up forming the popular Apple Computer Company along with his childhood

friend Steve Wozniak, who is an electronics expert. Jobs completely changed the electronics industry for the consumers.

When he died his net worth was more than $8.3 billion, and he certainly will be remembered forever.

6. Shawn Carter (Jay-Z)

Although Shawn Carter is more popular because of his musical exploits he has also shown many entrepreneurial characteristics in his career. In the early stages, when he was not successful and was not able to secure a single big record deal he would sell copies of his recording right from his car, but eventually, he did get to taste success and in 1995 managed to co-create his record label.

His great success in the music industry allowed Carter to invest in various other businesses like real estate, nightclubs, clothing brands, and also a sports managing agency wherein he represents many notable athletes. He has invested even in a champagne brand, has owned an important NBA franchise stake, and launched many signature cigars.

Even today Shawn Carter keeps on making music and keeps on touring and his net worth is $900m which is mainly because of his businesses and investments.

7. Dhirubhai Ambani

Dhirubhai Ambani was the most popular and enterprising Indian entrepreneur. His life is one of the best examples of rags to riches story. Dhirubhai Ambani undoubtedly rewrote the Indian corporate history and created a global corporate group. He was born on December 28, 1932, into a Modh family and his father was a school teacher.

Dhirubhai Ambani's entrepreneurial career began by selling "bhajias" in Mount Girnar to pilgrims over the weekends. After completing his matriculation, he moved to Aden, Yemen. He started serving there as an oil company clerk and gas-station attendant. In 1958 he returned to India with 50, 000 rupees and started his own textile trading company.

He also created the brand name Reliance, and in 1992 it became the first Indian company that began raising money in the global markets. Reliance also became the first ever Indian company to appear in the Forbes 500 list. The FICCI gave Dhirubhai Ambani the title of the Indian Entrepreneur of the 20th century. Forbes ranked him as the 138th richest person in 2002 with a net worth of $2.9bn.

8. Jack Ma

When talking about taking a hint hardly anyone can be as stubborn as Jack Ma. After graduating in the year 1988 (in which he had failed four times earlier) Jack found it really difficult to get work and was turned down by more than 30 companies, and 10 of his applications for a postgraduate course in the Harvard Business School were also rejected.

None of this could stop Jack Ma and luck also favoured him during his visit to his friends to the US in 1995. After he learned about the internet he successfully raised $20,000 to create an online directory for the Chinese businesses, and also took on web development projects for government organisations and Chinese companies.

Having gained so much experience, he went back to China and then created Alibaba, a very popular marketplace that we all know about. In 2014, he raised $25bn at the IPO stock exchange of Alibaba which is more than any other company ever earned.

Ma now is one of the wealthiest people in this world and has a net worth of about $43bn.

9. Oprah Winfrey

Oprah Winfrey's life is yet another rag to riches story. As you might know, Oprah is one of the 21st centuries' wealthiest African- American and has a net worth of more than $3 bn. Also, she is one of the most influential women in the whole world.

However, she was not always rich, not always lucky, and not always successful. She had a rough upbringing and was the kid of an unmarried teen. Her mother worked as a housemaid and she thus grew up in a bad financial state.

Her financial condition as a kid was so bad that she was teased in her school for wearing clothes made using potato sacks. Also, she had suffered from sexual abuse from her own family members, and she shared this with her TV viewers in one of the special episodes of her own show.

The first ever break of Oprah was a black local radio station show. Station managers were very happy with her passion and oration and this paved the way for Oprah to rank higher in bigger radio stations and finally, she made her appearance on the television as well.

10. Bill Gates

Bill Gates, without the slightest doubt, is one of the most popular entrepreneurs of this era. The second richest man in this world, Gates' net worth is more than $79bn. Before Jezz Bezos, the founder of Amazon become the richest man, Gates held the title 16 times in 21 years.

The co-founder of Microsoft, the largest PC software brand of the world, Gates had started showing great interest in computer programming right from a very young age. In fact, in all his free time he would just create programs in his teletype terminal computer that was donated by his school. Later, Gates created Microsoft and also developed the ever-popular Windows operating system.

Not only is he a great entrepreneur he is even popular for his philanthropic activities and donates a large sum of money to many scientific endeavors and charitable organizations.

In the year 2000, he even created the Bill and Melinda Gates Foundation to help reduce poverty, improve educational opportunities, enhance health care, and provide access to technology everywhere in the world.

Each of these entrepreneurs is successful, popular, and is minting money. What is more interesting is the fact that most of these big names had to start from the scratch, they had their own share of bad times, lack of money, and failure but that did not stop them, it only became an inspiration to work even harder and thus become what they are today.

Also, it serves as a lesson for all of us, if we are ready to put in all our efforts and dedication, we too might find our names in such lists very soon.

Top 10 Successful Entrepreneurs Around The World

There are a large number of entrepreneurs around the globe. Be that as it may, every one of these entrepreneurs can't move us. Some are successful, some fall flat and a few entrepreneurs are more than successful. They are our most helpful entrepreneurs. You have to tail them on the off chance that you need to star. They have certain characteristics, they have a superior identity, they are more productive than others.

So you have numerous things to gain from these best entrepreneurs on the planet. Have you at any point watched individuals in Third World nations and how they are simply the most ingenious and dependent entrepreneurs? Models would exchange business inside their locale, cultivating and bolstering nearby families, and making their own garments for individual utilize and exchange.

A considerable measure of families in the Third World have a locally situated business or the like. One can state they have to do this because of need, because of insignificant accessibility of occupations and their economy, be that as it may, I consider them to be individuals who have figured out how to make their conditions.

When you address entrepreneurs you can make certain of a certain something, these are individuals who have confidence in themselves. (Not limiting religion or confidence by any stretch of the imagination.) A business visionary does not generally know precisely how things will turn out however you can make certain they trust they will be successful at whatever they do.

So for what reason are extremely successful entrepreneurs great at such a significant number of things? Since they trust they can accomplish something and after that put their psyche and vitality into doing it. A business visionary is especially similar to a competitor. A successful competitor awakens at a young hour early in the prior day the vast majority hit the rest catch to go out for a run. There is no doubt as far as athletes can tell that they are responsible for their bodies and there is nobody who can beat them.

Preparing and tutoring, for the most part, go together making the time expected to devote to rehearse considerably to a greater degree a test. For expert competitors, the diversion of recently discovered riches and notoriety can be trying also.

So the competitors center around their game continually endeavoring to be the best. By secondary school, most competitors have chosen a game or two and train religiously consistently to enhance their abilities or decrease their time. This is a lifestyle which incorporates mentors and groups to help keep you on track. Beginning since early on there are camps and projects for each possible game. You can exceed expectations in any occasion or group which views your achievements as deserving of incorporation.

There are no associations for a youthful big shot. No mid-year camp for our little business visionary at the same time, there are numerous for an eight-year-old future prima ballet dancer. Those camps are busy to the point that I wager you know a few expert ballet dancers. So where does our young future mega well-off business person begin since there is no instructing staff at the center school?

So the future business visionary discovers openings and interests that they find entrancing. Investigating the circumstance all the more completely is never a little endeavor. Like the competitor, these are exceptionally determined, exceedingly capable, roused people who need to prevail at all that they attempt. They simply have not discovered what they will prevail at, because of the absence of structure which directs the competitor's reality.

Entrepreneurs go from diversion to leisure activity and game to don looking for significance just to miss the mark as a rule. So off to class where they inspire the staff as the hardest specialists and most devoted understudies, or they wind up scarcely graduating in light of the fact that they simply were not keen on anything enough to care the slightest bit about the subject.

So now the business visionary has numerous gifts and is a significant persuading sales representative. Enriched with appeal and mind, they more often than not give others a feeling of trust in their capacity. Wherever you look there are open doors for the business person. Achievement and disappointment resemble the competitor getting to the playoffs yet not making the finals, but rather there is no group for the business person to support or praise. Family aside, there is no group in a business person. It very well may be forlorn and difficult to confront overcome without realizing where to turn straight away. This does not keep going long for a business visionary. Regardless of what happens, this is simply one more disappointment that makes the business visionary more fit later on. Either a triumph or misfortune is essentially another exercise to be learned and considered for the following undertaking. Like a competitor who awakens after the huge annihilation, a business person is as yet a business visionary the following morning.

Champions, in any case, can be competitors or entrepreneurs. The competitor that turns into a boss might not have dependably been a hero but rather was dependably a competitor. The business visionary will either win or lose yet will dependably be a victor for having had a go at something new. Giving their best every time and hoping to discover gold when no decorations are being offered can be as troublesome as preparing for a game.

Entrepreneurs have faith in themselves seeing gold awards as the tricky metal ring to be looked for after and won. I trust this article must motivate you in you on the off chance that you are a novice. You get everything about these best 10 best entrepreneurs on the planet. You need to find out about those individuals who have officially won the core of billions of individuals. For what reason would you say you are pausing? In the event that you need to be a successful business person, you ought to pursue other uplifting entrepreneurs.

10 Most Successful Entrepreneurs in The World

A business person is a man who arranges and deals with a venture, particularly business. He/she is the greatest daring person. Entrepreneurs can go out on a limb in an urgent circumstance. There are billions of individuals around the globe. Numerous individuals need to accomplish something unique yet they would prefer not to go for broke. Life is extremely an undertaking of an Entrepreneur.

1. Steve Jobs
There is no man the world over who are not comfortable with Apple or different items from Apple. I have most likely that every one of the general population are extremely near MR. Steve Jos on the grounds that he is the most motivational entrepreneurs in this cutting-edge world.

Be that as it may, we extremely sad this incredible individual is no more with us. In any case, he will be with us perpetually for his incredible works. The life of MR Jobs was difficult, he has turned into the best business person by vanquishing every one of the deterrents. Employment was an American data technology business person and creator. He was the fellow benefactor, CEO of Apple Inc. Employments acquainted us with numerous world popular items like iPhone, iPad and more.

2. Bill Gates

Bill Gates is a standout amongst the most popular entrepreneurs in this advanced technology. Each individual everywhere throughout the world MR. Gates, he is the most extravagant individual all in our advanced universe. MR. Gates can be your motivation in the event that you simply begin. It is difficult to be one of them however you will get the least achievement in the event that you have a smart thought about the successful entrepreneurs.

Bill Gates is a US business tycoon, well-known business person, financial specialist and that's just the beginning. He is the prime supporter Microsoft, he and his companion Paul Allen created one of the greatest technology items maker organizations Microsoft.

Bill Gates is the key individual of Microsoft. He presented us with Windows, Office, servers, Skype, OneDrive, Windows Phone, diverse internet browsers, Xbox Live, LinkedIn and then some.

3. Larry Page And Sergey Brin

Larry Page and Sergey Brin are another most noteworthy innovators. Both are PC researchers and they are the most amazing entrepreneurs in this period. You think about Google the most groundbreaking and best internet searcher. Larry Page and

Sergey Brin are the of Google Inc.

These two persuasive people are our actual pioneers and they are motivating us to improve and new. Larry Page and Sergey Brin presented us with the biggest web search tool: Google, YouTube, Blogger, Android, Adsense, Google Plus, Google Chrome, Google Drive, many working and investigating programs.

4. Mark Zuckerberg

Zuckerberg is a standout amongst the most famous people far and wide. This isn't just the period of technology yet it is additionally the time of long range interpersonal communication site. Facebook is such a monstrous informal communication website that is a standout amongst the most vital items for web clients. Zuckerberg is an American developer, business person, and above all the prime supporter and CEO of Facebook.

MR. Zuckerberg is additionally associated with the most prominent informing application WhatsApp and another famous photograph sharing stage Instagram.

5. Larry Ellison

Larry Ellison is another uplifting individual for the general population of the world. The life of MR. Ellison was loaded with battles. Be that as it may, he could beat every one of the impediments in his lifestyle. Presently he has turned out to be a standout amongst the most incredible people in this technology part.

Ellison is additionally an American business visionary, software engineer, web mammoth, explorer, an altruism. He is the prime supporter of Oracle Corporation that makes database software, technology items, cloud designed frameworks and numerous other world-renowned items.

6. Jeff Bezos

Jeff Bezos is likewise an American businessperson, business tycoon, and speculator. He is the most imperative individual in the online business. MR. Bezos is the author, director and CEO of Amazon. A large number of individuals are working with Amazon.com. MR. Bezos has worked to perfection for every one of the general population simply like me who are doing for their job utilizing Amazon for their business purposes. So this man is extremely a genuine legend among us.

7. Richard Branson

Richard Branson is just the British native in this rundown. He is a successful business visionary, business financier, TV character, filmmaker and the sky is the limit from there. MR. Branson isn't just a single of the most rousing entrepreneurs for the

British individuals however he is likewise a notorious individual for us.

Branson is the organizer of the Virgin Group and this gathering controls in excess of 400 organizations. He is an extremely shrewd and extraordinary individual. You can pursue this individual on the off chance that you need to get genuine motivation.

8. Warren Buffett

Warren Buffett is the third most extravagant individual on the planet. Buffett is a standout amongst the best businesspeople and financial specialists. He is the second wealthiest individual in the United States of America. MR. Buffett is outstanding for his initiative of Berkshire Hathaway and Charlie Munger. We have numerous things to gain from this extraordinary individual.

9. Oprah Winfrey

Oprah Winfrey is the main lady on this rundown. She is extremely a notable identity for ladies as well as a persuasive figure for men. Conceived in a poor family yet she has just achieved the highest point of progress. Oprah Winfrey is an American media proprietor, representative, columnist, filmmaker, performing artist, giver and that's only the tip of the iceberg. She is notable for her multi-grant winning syndicated program The Oprah Winfrey Show.

10. Fred Smith

Fred Smith is another ground-breaking business visionary and business head honcho in the United States of America and also around the globe. His organization is serving everywhere throughout the world.

Smith is the organizer, administrator, president and CEO of FedEx. FedEx is initially known as Federal Express. It is a worldwide dispatch conveyance benefit.

In conclusion, these entrepreneurs are the one that runs the world because they have the capacity to do many things with their money. They can give the nations donations as well as doing charity work to the disadvantaged group in the world.

Top 10 Successful Products

Statistics show that over 80% of new businesses fail within two years. Lack of knowledge, inexperience and other reasons are among the common reasons why most online businesses are not successful.

However, on the flip side, other businesses start with the same resources under the same conditions, or even worse, but are still able to grow and establish themselves well. Yet again, there're lots of reasons why they succeed, one of them being the type of products they're dealing with.

A good choice of products has made several stores grow from mere buying and selling platforms into fully-fledged online stores. Although the market is dominated by several giant stores like Amazon and Aliexpress, a good choice of products will help you to make a kill in this industry.

A good selection of products will not only compel you to start making money at the comfort of your home but also enable you to grow your small online store into a mega-store. With that in mind, here are the top 10 successful products to include in your online store.

1. Phone Accessories

As the phone industry is developing exponentially day by day, so does the smartphone accessories industry! Screen protectors, Phone covers, phone grips, earphones, chargers, and other phone accessory products are introduced into the market on a daily basis.

Recently, this industry has brought in several innovative accessories that have now become essential for every smartphone user. According to predictive statistics, the smartphone accessories industry will grow to over $110 billion in the near future.

So, if you're looking for a top product to kick-start your e-commerce store, you can count on phone accessories. You'll be surprised by how these little things will give you massive profit margins.

2. Smartwatches

With the rise in popularity of smartphones and other 'smart' products, the market has an array of smartwatches, a product that has made our lives easier.

A few years ago, nobody could have thought of a wristwatch that can do more than just showing time, including telling us about our blood pressure, heart rate or even a GPS to guide us to our destination when travelling.

These are some common features that have made smartwatches to trend today. With this product trending for the past two years, why not include it in your online store to give it a sales boost?

3. Shapewear

Nowadays, we lead very static lifestyles which have made keeping our bodies in good shape hard to achieve. As a result, most people, especially women, are ready to sacrifice for anything that could make them feel better and more confident. This beauty crave made shapewear products to grow in popularity. These apparels are worn under any clothes where they painlessly shape an individual's body based on his/her definition of an ideal look.

What makes shapewear products worth considering is that they offer retailers lots of options: from selling them alongside women's fashion, lingerie, or even adding the product in a store that sells general apparel. Shapewear is available in different styles, sizes, and colors to meet all the needs and requirements of a diverse customer base.

The popularity of shapewear products particularly among women has made it appear in the top ten product list, making it a must- have product in your online store.

4. Facial Masks

As previously stated, women are always ready to give everything when it comes to beauty products and related techniques. As a matter of fact, even men have also started becoming conscious of their looks and the appearance of their skin. This has made facial masks a top-selling product that can give you higher profit margins.

These masks are available in various types, from the moisturizing ones to the deep cleansing ones, whitening masks, and even blackhead removers. The trend of using organic face masks that have minimal side effects has also made this product popular among teens, youth and even aging individuals. Adding these products to your online store will definitely give you massive profit margins.

5. Watches

Watches are brilliant items that can be worn to improve one's look, for communication purposes or even fitness monitoring purposes. Watches are made using different materials which include silver, gold, glass, metal, leather, plastic and rubber. Each material has its pros and cons. Over 1.5 billion watches are purchased each year globally, and this number keeps rising. While minimalist watches tend to be the most popular type of watch purchased by individuals, the reality is that we have other types of watches that are also doing well in the market.

Smartwatches, women's watches, and men's watches have also shown an increased number of sales over time. December seems to be the peak season for watch sales. While you can sustain a year-round sale with only a watch store, it's an excellent practice to stock the shop with other watch related accessories to get higher profits.

6. Athleisure

Athleisure is a transformation of sportswear into sports-lifestyle hybrid apparel. The baggy sweatpants and the high-cut shoes are now long gone. Popular brands like Nike and Adidas are on the forefront of manufacturing Athleisure wear, producing apparel and shoes that can be used for everyday wear, as well as making them comfortable and technologically-advanced to be used for training and sports.

Even though fashion trends are rapidly changing, athleisure is a fashion trend that is here to stay. Clothes that fall within this category include leggings, sports bras, sweatpants, tank tops, capris, shoes, and headbands, all available in different styles and colors. Athleisure don't do well when sold on their own, they should be sold together with other clothing apparel or sportswear.

7. Backpacks

A backpack is another top product that at least every family owns one or more. Backpacks are mostly sold as standalone products, with the peak season being around August when most kids are going back to school. Most backpack stores have several niches which include travel bags, school bags, or even fashion bags, allowing them to make nice profits while at the same time offering their customers a variety of bags.

Generally, women are the main consumers of handbags and backpacks. School children also purchase lots of them. Although men and travelers constitute a small percentage of the bags sold, they still add revenue to store owners.

8. Portable LED Projectors

Initially, projectors used to be huge and bulky. However, modern LED portable projectors have drastically redefined the industry. The market is flooded with powerful portable LED projectors that will not only fit in a small bag but also display pictures of a high-quality output than the initial quality of some of the best projectors of 2005.

As a result of its popularity, the portable led projector niche is expected to grow to over $3.44 billion by 2022. Some led projectors can easily be attached to any phone, making them desirable to carry around for people with presentations to make.

These projectors are available in different types and sizes which include laser projectors, handheld projectors, mini projectors, and more.

9. Night Masks

These night masks have also seen an increase in the number of sales on online stores. These masks offer an excellent solution to a tough problem: blocking out excess light to allow you to sleep more soundly.

Night masks are sold with different products including, beauty products, earphones, earplugs, pillows, and other accessories related to travelling. Most of these night masks are affordable at low cost.

Night masks are purchased by three main types of consumers: travelers, sensitive sleepers, and beauty enthusiasts. Travelers use sleep masks while sleeping on planes, or at night when sleeping in unfamiliar hotels. Sensitive sleepers use these masks to sleep in complete darkness since they find it difficult to sleep in bright rooms.

Beauty enthusiasts, in this case being women, use sleep masks for beauty rests. These women often go for masks that have anti-wrinkle materials like silk. These materials not only help them to look prettier but also help them to wake up feeling well rested. Night masks work well when sold with other products compared to when they're sold as standalone products.

10. Maternity Dresses

The maternity dress industry is a multi-billion-dollar industry since the maternity growth rate grows by at least 2% on a yearly basis.

Maternity fashion stores are doing well in this industry, with most of them expanding to other verticals which include baby products and even wedding accessories.

You could sell these dresses with books on pregnancy, prenatal workout videos, and courses on preparing first-time pregnant women for a new phase in life, which is motherhood.

These digital products could even be part of your sales funnel for your physical products store. With all these said, the top ten products are not necessarily the best products for building your e-commerce store.

There's a wide gap between the top 10 products and the best items to sell on your online store. If you want to make it in this industries, there's only one possible way to succeed: specialization. Starting a new store and including all the products mentioned above is not something most beginners can do.

Chapter 1- Strength

"What doesn't kill you, makes you stronger"
- Kelly Clarkson

When people hear about the term strength on most occasions including job interviews, they mostly think that it's an obvious and easy term with a simple explanation. Apart from job seekers, people in sports and entrepreneurs also ask themselves this question to improve their performance and businesses respectively.

What is a strength?
Strength is defined as the area in your personal life and business where you're incredibly efficient, and it's easy to achieve success in a particular field.

Strengths might include the following:
Experience in a particular field- web design, writing, programming, painting impressively among others.

Soft skills- Characterized by your relationship with others. Includes social skills, interpersonal skills.

Hard skills- includes professional skills in most cases like medical expertise. Formal education and training- training seminars, mentoring among others.

Strength in sports

For optimum performance in all sports, strength fitness training is necessary. The strength is developed with other fitness components to match every sport's physical demands.

Benefits of strength training in sports:

1. Muscle mass preservation. Strength training is essential to the preservation of muscle mass . This helps in improving the overall performance in every sport.

2. Enhanced coordination and balance. Performing routine strength training help in maintaining proprioception and balance at higher levels for years to come and also prevent the falls and injuries that hasten the decline one's overall activity.

3. Increases your workout options. For those who have been pursuing a single endurance sport for some time, there are chances that they have a well-developed aerobic capacity. On the other hand, they potentially have an underdeveloped musculoskeletal system for other things other than their chosen sport. The underdeveloped strength of the upper body is prevalent and can limit the activity options available to the outside of your great athletic endeavors.

4. Become a well-rounded sportsman. Focusing on one sport isn't a bad thing, although it limits your expansion to other horizons when it comes to training.

However, strength training is essential for injury prevention and also enhances a more consistent pattern in your specific sports training.

Examples of strength for some sports include:
For powerlifters, their strength should be developed to lift maximum weight in each competitive lift.

A gymnast should develop isometric strength and explosive isotonic to execute skills unique to the gymnastics.

A rower should be strong enough in order to sustain submaximal, rhythmic and muscular efforts in the entire duration of the course.

A wrist wrestler should be isotonically and isometrically strong enough in order to overcome the opponent's resistance in a single, maximum sustained effort.

Strength in business
It's common for people to compare themselves

with others, and feel either inferior or superior towards them based on their weaknesses or strengths.

In order to operate successfully in the dynamic market, businesses need to plan their strategies and objectives around their strengths and look for measures to downplay their weaknesses. As a business owner, your strengths are the things you can use to grow more and more.

The key strengths of successful businesses include reliability, competence, openness, and compassion. Importance of knowing your business strengths

1. Understanding your strengths gives you a better chance of knowing how your business is functioning. You'll also know the areas to monitor in order to maintain your revenue and profits.

2. Understanding your strengths also enables you to stay ahead in many things. For instance, if your business is dealing with multiple products, then you'll be able to know a single product that you can work on only and get good returns.

3. Business growth. Your strengths are a significant determinant in business growth. Simply knowing what you're good at will enable you to aim higher and achieve more in your business.

4. Understanding your strengths will also give you a clear picture of what steps to take from what may be holding you back.

If your business has some challenges that you see some possible solutions of overcoming them, then you can quickly implement them to get out of trouble and be successful.

There are wonderful things you can achieve if you understand your true potential and the things you're capable of doing. Some of the examples of strength in business include product innovation, highly efficient, excellent customer service, low-cost manufacturing, and strong employee attitudes.

CHAPTER 2 - SPEED

"EARLY BIRD CATCHES THE WORM" - UNKNOWN
(This was what my grandma used to tell us all the time)

Speed is the rate at which something happens and is dependent on acceleration, speed maintenance and maximal speed of movement. For the movement speed, power and strength are required in totality. Apart from movement speed, there are other many areas where speed can be utilized too including the businesses.

Speed in sports

Speed is a significant fitness component that is very important in most sports. In most cases, track and field, sprinters, cyclists, sprint swimmers, and speed skaters require speed and take it as an essential aspect of fitness. In other sports like team field sports, speed also plays a vital role in the overall fitness profile. However, speed training is a must for most of the sports which require movement for success.

Benefits of speed training

1. Increase in muscle power. It involves an increase in muscle power of the sports-person through both speeds in the starting and stopping function. All exercises become much easier with the explosive force behind each repetition, which makes speed training ideal for athletes and powerlifters who perform rapid movements and run respectively.

2. Increased agility. Speed training increases agility, movement speed, and exercise technique. The twitch muscle ability also increases over time. Some exercises in speed training include the addition of speed enhancers or weighted resistance in order to force fast twitch muscles into overdrive.

3. Improved performance. It generally increases the athlete's good performance ability. With some exercises like agility drills, skipping, sprinting or hopping motions, athletes gain muscle memory and experience in motions and exercises that happen during a game or practice situations.

4. Improved oxygen delivery into the muscles. In simple terms, your muscles will have the ability to function effectively will less amount of oxygen.

5. Gives a mental edge. Speed training is essential in giving a mental edge as one tries to push and challenge himself to his body limits. This offers mental toughness and a greater advantage in games and also when training.

6. Increases your stamina. The ability to run with an even pace without getting tired at the end.

Speed in business

It's common knowledge that business owners and entrepreneurs must think fast in order to survive. However, you can't underestimate the importance of speed in business. With today's society, businesses have to do all it takes in order to stay relevant. Below are the top reasons why speed is important in business:

1. Going ahead of your competitors. With the much-growing competition in business, there's a need to stay ahead of your competitors so that success is attained. Every business owner out there is working harder from day to day to take the next step quickly.

If you can't move quickly, then your competitors will overtake you and lessen your market share. They won't worry leaving you down there if you make decisions at a slower pace. Ensure you accelerate up-to a point where you're in front of others and try to maintain.

2. The audience expects it. In today's business world, the consumers are ever waiting for the next big thing from different businesses. For instance, every year the consumers are eager to see the new kind of phones that a particular company releases.

Consumers aren't satisfied with the status quo, and thus they need something more. However, every business must move with speed to satiate their appetites simply because the prospective customers won't have qualms about moving to other products or services.

Regardless of whether you're running a media company, a bank, or a retail company, it's important to leverage IT to assist you to innovate and evolve your business otherwise it will die. The choice is simple as to whether you're going to or you'll allow your competitors crush you in the market.

3. Learning faster results in faster evolution. As businesses learn to move faster, they tend to evolve faster to the point of near exponential growth.

Generally, the speed at which an entrepreneur moves is majorly determined by his ability to balance the scalable infrastructure against the low overhead costs. With this, standing out and fulfilling expectations becomes very easy.

4. Creates a speed culture. The culture of speed is naturally formed when you learn to move faster and maintain speed. With all business aspects moving faster in their implementation, the efficiency and innovation go through the roof, reducing your competition and bringing more potential customers.

In conclusion, no business in any field can go ahead with a slow culture. Entrepreneurship involves moving forward and pushing innovations ahead.

CHAPTER 3 – STAMINA

Stamina is the energy and strength that allows one to sustain physical or mental effort for an extended period. To endure discomfort or stress when performing a particular activity, then you should increase your stamina. This also reduces exhaustion and fatigue.

Stamina in sports
Endurance training is a way of exercising that improves the ability of the body to withstand an activity for extended periods. Generally, if you want to increase your stamina, then endurance training is the best form of exercise. Endurance training involves training the aerobic energy system as opposed to the anaerobic system.

The benefits of increased physical stamina in sports:
1. Physiology. If you increase your stamina, your muscles will work more efficiently. However, endurance training increases the lung capacity and thus allowing one to take more oxygen after breathing. Additionally, it strengthens the heart which results in pumping oxygen faster to your fibers.

2. Increase in bone density. Endurance training gives the bones extra support and also increases their density. This also assists in preventing osteoporosis. If this condition has been in your family since the past, you may consider taking this.

Question to ask ourselves: What is the point of being successful if we don't get to enjoy it because of sickness then die early?

When training, the body releases the growth hormones into the bloodstream which allows the bones to build better density.

3. Enhanced immune system. Regardless of how strong you are, your body can sometimes fail to defend yourself against diseases. However, endurance training can improve the immune system by producing extra proteins required for the production of antibodies and white blood cells.

4. Enhanced metabolism. People grow bigger as they grow older as a result of the decrease in metabolic processes. Due to this, the body can burn fewer calories in the form of round bellies. Endurance training helps this problem through muscle mass addition.

As the muscle mass increases, more calories are burned through the production of the necessary acids required to expand and break down the calories consumed.

Stamina in business
Entrepreneurial stamina is the inner power of enduring physical and mental fatigue, distress, difficulty, and hardship. To maintain business growth, every business owner requires unfaltering entrepreneurial stamina. In most cases, people look at the successful entrepreneurs and attribute their success to their social connections or a single brilliant idea.

While these are key ingredients to success, the main ingredient of making it as an entrepreneur involves both mental and physical stamina which can be attained through working out. Most entrepreneurs have busy schedules which limit them from working out.

It's important to keep the physical fitness commitments since they'll help you focus on the growth of your business better.

Why should entrepreneurs work out?

1. Relieves stress. A company comes with many challenges and stresses. However, you must adopt a stress relief plan to avoid losing your ambition or entering into a depression. The entrepreneurs make frequent business trips which make it stressful. Having a good workout plan will help you in relieving stress. If you're having a difficult presentation or a conference, then having a light workout is necessary for clearing your mind.

2. Maintaining a work-life balance. If you adopt a routine exercise plan, you will maintain a healthy work-life balance which prevents either business or family suffering. Economic welfare isn't total welfare. You must schedule time for business, time for your family and time for yourself. You can use your time to work out so that you stay fit and healthy.

3. Energy and productivity. Regular working out will give you more energy throughout the day. If your business is new, then a lot of energy is required to perform all activities required for growth and making new customers. If you have more energy, it's very easy to face all business challenges of the day confidently and aggressively.

4. Improves creative thinking skills. Entrepreneurs should maintain a creative thought process in order to evolve with technology, industry competitors and marketing trends.

Performing exercises in order to be fit can assist in bringing innovative solutions for increasing efficiency, solving product defects and presentation delivery issues in your workforce.

Entrepreneurs with difficulty in solving problems, focusing and being creative will likely forget to take care of bodies and minds. After long working days, make sure you perform some exercises to become fresh and clear all your thoughts.

CHAPTER 4 – STRATEGY

A PLAYER WITH BETTER STRATEGY WINS THE GAME. A BUSINESS PERSON WITH BETTER STRATEGY GETS BETTER RESULTS.

A **strategy** is a plan of action that is designed to achieve long- term goals. In sports, a strategy is essential for achieving a competitive edge as a result of doing things differently. On the other hand, strategies are required in businesses which majorly involve being different and anticipation of future events in order to respond and react proactively. Irrespective of whether its sports or business, each team will work in different ways that reflect their capabilities, goals, and assumptions.

Strategy in sports
Sports play a significant role in physical activity and also having fun. If you engage in sports regularly, then chances are that you need to get better on the activity you do. Regardless of the sport you play, you must have a strategy on how to improve your skills and performance.

Below are some top tips on how to strategize yourself in order to make a change in your performance:

1. Set your goals. Before you start to practice in order to get better at your favorite sport, think about your goals. This will help you to focus on your training and ensure you know what you want after all. Set attainable goals so that you won't quit as a result of lofty options.

For instance, if today you're able to run 1 mile in 10 minutes, you can set a goal of running 1 mile in 8 minutes in the next five months. It's easy to formulate a plan for your training if you have a concrete goal.

2. Formulate a plan. It's possible to stick to any goals you have set for a particular sport if you formulate a reasonable plan. The plan must include the goals you have to reach, specific drills or even training session times. However, a gradual improvement will make you motivated and not fatigued to a point where you may quit. You can use sports magazines, trainers, coaches or even friends to formulate plans.

3. Stretch your muscles. While there are many opinions regarding the benefits of stretching, it's true that it can improve the range of motion. This helps sportspeople including athletes to perform better and also minimizes the risk of injury. Additionally, stretching leads to increased blood flows to the muscles and improve flexibility, both which makes one better in sports.

4. Build self-confidence. Having confidence in your ability and skills can provide a foundation for sports improvement. If you meet your set goals and continue to maintain, while building confidence in your skills, then you'll be in a better position to do better in sports.

5. Proper nutrition. Different sports have different nutritional requirements. However, eating a diet that is rich in vitamins and nutrients will help fuel your training sessions and get better at your favorite sport. The foods with moderate fat amounts and high amounts of carbohydrates are a perfect option to fuel your workout.

Strategy in business

Business growth can sometimes be a frustrating and challenging process. Regardless of how experienced, talented or proficient you are as a business owner, business development can be draining your funds, energy and your desire to achieve your immediate plans for your business. Business growth plays a crucial role in maximizing your business's potential in revenue enhancement. However, to achieve success, you need a growth strategy.

Below are some strategies that can lead to business growth:

1. Leveraging. It's essential for every business to look for ways of leveraging everything they do in many ways. The first question to ask before starting a new service, introducing a new product or an innovative idea revolves around how you will be able to leverage it. If you think critically, all business aspects you're engaged in have the opportunity to be leveraged in many ways.

2. Relationship building. Relationships are critical aspects of business growth. It's essential to build high trust relationships with all your clients who deal with your business in any way, form or shape.

The more clients know you, how you work, your values and ethics, the higher the chances of these clients referring other people to your business.

3. Clarity. You should have understandable metrics of your staff as well as clear job descriptions. It may sound silly; although the clearer these pieces are, the higher the productivity your business will have. Growth is as a result of increased performance.

4. Infrastructure. Your business infrastructure includes planning, budgets among other business pieces involved in creating and maintaining the different parts of your business.

5. Learning. Learn day by day to find out why each move or action didn't work out as expected. Simply because your marketing initiative succeeded today doesn't mean that it will next time. Take time and analyze what made it succeed.

In conclusion, these are some top strategies for business growth. Additionally, ensure there's effective communication within your business.

CHAPTER 5 - SKILLS

A **skill** is an expertise required to perform a particular task. There are numerous skills that can assist you to succeed in many aspects of your life whether it's work, school or in sports.

Examples of skills include:
- Leadership and management skills, i.e. diplomacy, interviewing, problem-solving, among others.
- Organizational skills, i.e. project management, scheduling, multitasking among others
- Sports skills, i.e. flexibility, power, precision, performing repetitive drills, tactics, teamwork among others.

Skills in sports
They are required in a very progressive sequence. However, different people will acquire different skills at different rates. There are some steps to master new skills in sports as follows:

1. Don't start where you think, start where you are. This is the first step of mastering a new skill. You should work just from where you are and not where you think you should be. This will give you motivation that you can quickly master that sports skill without any difficulties.

2. Develop a growth mindset. Ensure you develop a growth mindset which means replacing the negative phrases in your mind with the positive ones. Just believe that you can acquire a particular skill. Provided that you're given enough time, direction, and you are patient, then you'll be able to do all things you think are impossible.

3. Keep practicing. We all know that practice makes perfect. Many people have an inner feeling that it's not lack of practice, but they are not making any progress. However, the truth is that improvement can sometimes be hard to see. Ensure you keep on practicing, and you'll acquire that skill of interest at your own pace.

4. Understand your learning process. Different people will learn differently and at different paces. This step can go on for some days, weeks, or even months depending on the intensity of the skill or capability of the person. If you're struggling to know a particular skill, ensure that you examine it to know if you're using the right technique.

5. Seek expert advice. Most people are willing to seek professional advice, although others aren't ready to take advantage of it. Being open to advise from the experts is only possible if you've embraced the first step to the fourth one and no positive change or impact is seen. An expert will make you see some significant changes and make significant progress.

Skills in business

Having a successful business demands more than just passion. Majority of the businesses fail just because the business owner is unable to translate his passion into practical business skills. Business success demands more than just hard work, expertise and resilience.

You require a set of fundamental business skills. Below are some essential skills that will help your business to grow and succeed:

1. Communication skills. Proper communication skills are essential in every business. This is because it's through communication whereby a business is able to operate without any delays or failure to meet deadlines.

2. Negotiation skills. Negotiations form part of our daily business life. However, formal negotiation skills can be learned through practice and experience. People who negotiate more frequently tend to be more skilled than those who don't participate. On the other hand, experienced people know what to say and what not to say. The key is to understand how to develop a win-win approach when negotiating with all parties.

3. Strategic planning skills. This is the process of defining a business's strategy and making timely decisions on resource allocation. The objective is to protect your business's future performance in a specific time frame as defined in your business plan.

4. Leadership skills. Leadership is a critical management skill which is geared towards motivating a group of people to ascertain a common goal. It also involves taking charge, assembling, mobilizing, and motivating teams. The objective is to create long-term relationships with customers, prospects, employees, and investors.

5. Analytical skills. In today's business world, the workplace is becoming technologically advanced and complex. This is the reason why analytical thinking is needed. Analytical thinking majorly involves the ability to assess the state of your business, what to do to close the gaps between the present and the future and the position you want your business in the future. The key here is understanding how to gather, evaluate and review data required formulate compelling arguments.

6. Sales and marketing skills. Involves establishing sales and marketing techniques and policies, pricing and advertising techniques that are essential in business growth. Ability to understand your target market, competition, and industry trends is very critical when developing your marketing strategy.

The key is to understand how to communicate a compelling message to your target audience in order to generate more sales, which in turn translates to more profits.

Other skills required in business include team building skills, general management skills, cash flow management skills, financial management skills, and time management skills.

CHAPTER 6 - SPIRIT

A SMALL CHANCE TO WIN IS STILL A CHANCE. IF YOU GIVE UP, THERE WILL BE NO MORE CHANCE.

Fighting spirit or determination. One can never talk about a fighting spirit especially in sports without mentioning one John Stephen Akwhari. In 1968 Olympic Games, Akwhari pushed to finish the race with severe injuries. Though he did not win the race, John taught the world a critical lesson, the need for a fighting spirit in everything one does. Despite not winning the race, his tolerance and combative spirit earned him a place in the hearts of many.

Business and sports are not for the feeble-hearted but rather individuals who are able to cope with the various destructive situations and the competitive world. The business world itself is full of challenges and entrepreneurs who made it had to fight some big obstacles in order to be in their current positions.

A sports context is thus not an exception to this. Your competitors can be almost impossible to beat and therefore a positive spirit is such a major requirement to deal with such a situation. A fighting spirit is the best tool you can use to emerge victoriously.

Discussed herein are some of the key benefits of fighting spirit in the two fields mentioned before.

- **It instills a winning mentality**. One major boon of a fighting spirit is that it gives you the feeling that you can topple down every challenge. Instead of viewing yourself as an underdog, this spirit instills the feeling of a winner. The famous Gatlin win against Usain Bolt could never have been if Gatlin never felt that he could fight and win against Bolt. Similarly, even during the thickest of times, such a spirit in business always gives you the feeling that even the worst market movements can be endured.

- **Internal Motivational Factor**. A fighting spirit gives you the need to conquer. Identifying your strength and your specific goals is such a great idea that triggers your success. The goals play a significant role in encouraging and motivating you more to work more each time you have a chance to achieve your desires. Working towards unspecified interests and goals definitely leads to failures and it is thus very important to understand what you actually need to establish. That internal feeling of a deficiency in conquest acts as a driving force. This spirit will thus enable you to hold the fort even in the worst of times. Your principal goal under this spirit is to win and you will never give up.

- **See positives in weaknesses.** Have you ever noticed that when you want to win, you forget all your flaws and work as a whole unit rather than an individual divided into strengths and differences? Adapt to the spirit of a fighter and your weakness will turn into your strengths.

You may easily fight your weaknesses by maximizing your attention and focus on your strengths. It very easy to fail if you focused on your incapability and if you treated yourself as a failure. Developing a positive attitude and spirit towards your weaknesses makes a very big difference between your success and failures and it is thus important to consider the idea.

- **Acts as Mean of Self Evaluation.** In the course of fighting to achieve your goals, you need a mean to evaluate if you are still on track. One meaning can be a fighting spirit. It helps you know by how much are you away from achieving your target. Before you even begin facing the obstacles on your to achieving your dreams, you prepare a schedule. At any given moment, if you are not in the required stage of execution of your plan, the fighting spirit in you will automatically detect it and help you stay on track.

- **You essentially need one.** With the numerous challenges in the two fields, you certainly need a fighting spirit. It is almost guaranteed that without one, you are bound to fail. Doubtlessly, you need a fighting spirit if you are to achieve what you want in sports or business.

Many of the much-celebrated sportsmen and businessmen in the world faced a lot of challenges before success came. A look at the likes of Dangote, Steve Jobs in business and the likes of Wyde Van Niekerk in sports necessitate the need of a fighting spirit. Adopt one and you will surely soar high in your business or sports career.

CHAPTER 7 - SELF-CONFIDENCE

"WHAT YOUR MIND CONCEIVE, YOU WILL ACHIEVE" - UNKNOWN

Self-confidence is basically the ones believe in their capabilities or the skills required in accomplishing a particular task. It is a psychological aspect that is highly required in the performance of any activity especially in the field of sports since it highly determines the success of a player in a particular game.

If a player does not believe in their abilities and capabilities, then it simply means that they cannot succeed in whatever they are doing even if they have the abilities to do so. If you are confident in whatever you are doing, you will definitely develop some positive emotions, and you will be highly motivated and focused on success.

Self-confidence is thus an important contributor to success in sports and business. Psychological factors contribute to approximately 90% of success in sports, and there is, therefore, a need to ensure that all athletes develop this aspect to improve their performances.

This chapter, therefore, outlines some techniques to gain self- confidence in different sporting activities and the associated benefits of developing confidence in sports and in business as well.

Techniques to gain self-confidence in various sporting activities: A player needs to fully understand what they are capable of and also identify what limits them from their success. This can easily be achieved by careful examination of their past record performances. When a player realizes that they once performed well in their previous sporting activities, it is easy to reassure themselves that they can as well do it again.

Athletes should thus empower themselves with these positive experiences to work on their past failures so as to keep succeeding. For instance, if a footballer missed a score in a previous game, then they should not treat themselves as losers but rather improve their scoring skills so as to win in the next match. This particular technique thus plays a significant role in helping the athlete develop a positive attitude towards their performances.

Self-talk is also another technique that may greatly help an athlete in improving their performances. In this case, one needs to honestly evaluate themselves while identifying their strengths as well as their weaknesses in the particular sporting activities that they engage in. These meditations should entail a detailed evaluation of past performances, their hard work, talents, and determination towards their success. An athlete should undertake this program seriously in order to develop a strong belief in their abilities towards success.

This technique can thus be very important especially when a player is heading to peak performance and should thus be taken seriously.

Self-confidence can also be achieved through imagery procedures. This is a mental state that involves creating positive images of your performances. This process helps you focus on the current or future activities and hence avoiding you from figuring out on your past failures which could as well discourage you from your performing well.

Benefits of self-confidence in sporting and business activities:

1. Self-confidence helps athletes to develop greater potential. Being confident in your abilities helps to develop a positive attitude towards your strengths and hence impacting on your performance potentials. An athlete will definitely score higher if they strongly believe in their capabilities and as well work hard on their abilities towards success.

2. Cope with negative attitudes. An athlete can easily manage their negative feelings on their abilities by acknowledging their strengths and efforts in their sporting activities. Focusing on the present time's activities and believing that they could win as they had done it in the previous matches can help them handle their negative ideas on their capabilities which could have resulted from failures in previous performances.

3. Improves one's efforts and motivation. When you are confident in whatever you are doing, you are able to increase your efforts and motivation in performing a particular task. Athletes who are confident in their performances tend to be highly encouraged and motivated to win in their matches.

4. Helps to handle intimidation. Being intimidated is such a difficult situation to handle especially if you do not have some doubts about your abilities. The situation can quite traumatize you if you do not manage it quickly and this can highly impact on your performances. If an athlete is able to develop strong believe in themselves it is easy to handle negative threats posed to them.

5. Overcome fear. Self-confidence helps a player overcome fear and negative thoughts about their skills when preparing for peak performance. When they are sure of what they are capable of, it is easy to handle such feelings and focus on their success.

Increasing your self-confidence will not only help you achieve your goals but also improve your leadership capabilities at home and even in your professional levels. An athlete should consider increasing their confidence levels in order to score higher and as well improve their performances.

CHAPTER 8 - SELF-CONTROL

YOUR WORST ENEMY IS YOUR SELF. MY WORST ENEMY IS MY SELF.

Self-control is quite an essential mental aspect in every sporting activity. Being able to handle effectively or carry out your duties leads to positive results due to better decision making.

In a sports context, self-control does not only entail an athlete's ability to control their impulses or desires but also affecting on higher deals and empowering the positive ideas towards achieving higher goals in the present time and also in the future. Most at times, athletes are faced with different challenging issues related to their decision making abilities on their sporting activities which as a result affects their sporting performances.

An adequate possession of self-control resources is thus required to handle such issues. Various sporting aspects such as cognitive, emotional and behavioral trends highly need to be controlled positively by the athletes in order to trigger optimal performances in their matches. At times withstanding some dominant behaviors or relieving distress situations in a competitive environment could be very difficult to most players but trying to adhere to some of these situations even to minor levels could make a big difference. Exercising self-control traits by little amounts can ultimately lead to amazing results of one's ability to fully get control of their activities.

How does self-control works?
Self-control can be viewed as a process in which a person tries to overrule some dominating situations in order to achieve the desired goal. This process is referred to as the strengths model whereby the operations of self-control depend on a restrained energy resource.

When individuals try to engage in self-control aspects, some of this energy supply is used and as a result, leave them in a depleted state for a certain period. If one tried to exercise self-control aspects later after a short time, the results seem to be poor than if you as compared to if they had not formerly exercised the aspect. This process can thus be related to how a muscle works. Just the way one may get exhausted after performing certain duties is the exact way in which self- control operates.

The acts of self-control can thus affect one's performance in their sports, and there is thus a need to control one's behaviors to avoid poor performances. For example, an athlete has to maintain low anxiety levels in a sporting environment in order to maintain a greater focus on the sporting activity in which he is currently carrying out.

Being mindful about your activities can be a good step to control your behaviors.

This approach is widely used by athletes to accept their situations that come their way even if they do not seem to appease them. Through this, one is able to focus and concentrate on the major sporting events rather than dwelling on some minor activities that distract their attention.

Careful meditation and observation of various things and events surrounding them can also play an essential role in helping them to understand the important activities that require more attention and hence redirect their efforts and focus to such activities.

Benefits of self-control in sport and business:
- **Increases the chances of success.** Being able to manage some distrustful desires or behaviors increases the chances of success. Self-control enables an athlete to identify the important areas that require much attention and hence put more efforts on them and hence increase the winning chances as a result.

- **Leads to better decision making.** Exercising self-control helps to arrive at better decisions amongst athletes since the mind only focuses on simple processes without engaging conflicting situations of stress or anxiety among other distractive behaviors.

- **Improves one's focus and concentration in a given activity.** Negative thoughts or feelings highly impact on an athlete's performances, and if the situation is not managed easily, poor results can be realized. Self-control enables a player to exert all their energies on the particular tasks that they are involved in and hence helping them to achieve the best results of their abilities.

- **Promotes equivalence.** Practicing self-control promotes congruence even in a sporting context. Athletes are able to relate similar activities and hence identify and focus on the important tasks rather than engaging in two conflicting situations.

From the above discussions, it is very clear that self-control is an important aspect in the life of every athlete and it is thus the responsibility of every player to adopt the relevant skills required to maintain it in order to achieve the desired goals.

CHAPTER 9 - SELF-DISCIPLINE

WHATEVER YOU DO IN YOUR LIFE, AS LONG AS YOU ARE NOT DOING ANYTHING WRONG OR STUPID, YOU HAVE NOTHING TO WORRY ABOUT.

Success is a function of many factors, with one of them being what you do when you are alone. In sports, if you only train and eat the recommended foods when your coach is around, you are bound to fail. Similarly, if you only work hard and behave in an ethical manner when your boss or client is around, you may not have a bright career in business. Every day, we hear of famous business persons who wake up early before their employees. Occasionally, we see how sportsmen rise early for a morning jog or training. This constitutes what is called self-discipline.

Self-discipline is a prerequisite to success in sports and business. Possession of self-discipline is such a significant achievement in the life of every individual. Almost every activity that we engage in our entire lives requires the principle of self-discipline in order to accomplish our goals. If you need to run your business successfully, accomplish a particular task effectively or even improve your overall performances in your workplace then think no more than just developing self-discipline skills in your actions. Self-discipline is the link between your set goals and the achievement of those targets, and you definitely need it to succeed in your endeavors.

There are numerous benefits from exercising self-discipline. Discussed herein are some of the notable benefits of self- discipline you will have to take advantage of if you employed the self-discipline skill.

Proper Time Management. Punctuality and proper time management are the pillars on which successful businesspersons and sportsmen build their success on. With self-discipline, you are able to remain within the required path without supervision. While friends are making merry, you will be actively pursuing your dreams.

Stick to your goals. Sometimes it could be very difficult to withstand failures or losses in big matches for athletes, and some elements are highly required to control such situations in order to stick in your lanes towards achieving the set targets.

Meditate regularly. An athlete will definitely need to frequently meditate on his abilities and weaknesses and how to easily overcome their weaknesses using their strengths. This is not easy to achieve if self-discipline is not developed in them.

Promotes Ethics. Self-disciplined people know that there is no difference from being a professional to being unprofessional. Even in parties, you will always conduct yourself like a professional. The recurrent practice builds unquestionable professionalism in you. You observe work ethics and being ethical becomes a part of you. Being able to accomplish your plans is not a simple task, and you really need some force to push you towards the goals. Self-discipline is among the top principles you cannot ignore in your efforts towards achieving your desires. The business environment and the sport's world are not at any time an exemption to this principle. For an athlete to focus on their events and emerge as winner, a higher level of self-discipline is very crucial.

Self-discipline plays a significant role in helping you stick to your objectives despite the challenges that you could be going through in order to gain some positive results in your goals. It empowers one to conquer some challenges that come your way in regard to achieving your goals. Laziness, addictions and some dominant desires are some of the things that one finds it hard to away with. However, with self- discipline in place, all these challenges are easily handled. Self- discipline gives one the ability to persevere during the difficult times when destruction and temptations come their way. It is thus very clear that we need to acknowledge the need for it in every situation that we want to conquer.

It is very ironical how many people confess the significance of self- discipline in their daily activities but does not spend any time trying to develop or reinforce it in their lives. It is such an important element in the success of every business person and should not be assumed whatsoever.

Acquiring this skill and maintaining it all through your activities needs frequent training and exercises to reinforce it. It is such an important ingredient towards success, and you definitely cannot afford losing it. Identify what you need to achieve and ensure your behaviors are directed in such a way towards your goals.

Always remember, you don't need a degree to have a self- discipline. All you need is to decide whether you will practice it or not.

CHAPTER 10 - SELF-IMPROVEMENT

WHAT WE ARE TODAY, IS THE RESULT OF WHAT WE DID YESTERDAY. WHAT WE ARE TOMORROW, DEPENDS ON WHAT WE DO TODAY.

We excitedly watch as athletes break records, footballers score supernatural goals and rugby players score numerous tries. We have even read different articles on the famous Bill Gates and Steve Jobs. However, we have never paused and asked ourselves what makes them the best in what they do to succeed in all their jobs. Undoubtedly, being the best in any particular event requires a great deal of self-improvement and sacrifice.

Self-improvement calls for perseverance during the difficult times in the business and also avoiding any destructive activities that could hinder you from achieving your goals. Self- improvement is the main key to a bright career in any field ranging from running our homes, expanding businesses and winning in international matches among other activities that require your attention so as to succeed. It helps you grow in every aspect of your life, and it is thus very essential in our day to day activities.

In a sporting environment, the self-improvement principle is highly required to create a stronger relationship amongst the players, control the different behavior of your players and also improve the overall performance of all athletes in the match.

This idea of self-improvement has been acknowledged by many through different people find it hard to hold it for longer durations. If they possess the skill, it only takes a shorter period before they lose it again.

Discussed below are some of the significant benefits of self-improvement in sports that could help you understand what you could gain if you fully acquired the skill in your activities.

• **Leads to self-awareness**. Focus on self-improvement will enable you to know yourself better. It will help you identify your strengths as well as your weaknesses, and this will be of great help in enabling you to understand what you actually expect in your performances.

You will also be able to understand how to use your strengths to overcome your weaknesses so as to avoid failures. This will also aid you in finding solutions to your problems. The strengths could also be exploited them to the maximum for the success of your sports performances and even in your business.

- **Builds character.** With the self-awareness derived from self- improvement, you understand how you can interact with other people. Awareness about how certain behaviors impact on others is a key to a good character. Such a character is gradually advanced to a leader and winning spirit.

- **Development of the right attitude.** Unlike focusing on means to beat others, in self-improvement, you focus on doing your best and hope that at your best, you can win. Opponents and competitors do not seem rivals but rather people out to bring the best out of you. You also learn to respect others and appreciate the talents in them.

- **Acquisition of Important Life Skills and Virtues.** During self- improvement, you are able to learn humility and learn from others. You also develop a sense of self-esteem and appreciate your self-advancement. In short, you are able to develop the right attitude, attributes, and character of a winner.

Research shows that sportsmen and businesspersons who focus on self- improvement end up being at levels that they would not have achieved if they focused on beating opponents. This a true phenomenon as depicted herein. Adopt self-improvement, and you will doubtlessly take your sports career or business to the next level that you have always dream of.

In conclusion, sports or business, what doesn't kill us make us stronger. Life is like computer games, we need to finish every stage and get the experience and strength needed for the next stage. It's better to fail and fall hundred times whilst still on the ground than fail and fall once when you are on top.

TOP 10 SUCCESS BOOKS

If you are looking to be successful in life, then you might want to walk in the shoes of the successful people. There is no better way of doing this than reading their success stories. Most successful people have opened up into their success by publishing books about the same. So if you are looking to be successful, then you might want to read these success books. Here are 10 success books you might want to read.

1. Millionaire next door
Millionaire next door is one of the best selling success books in the world. If you are thinking of being successful, this is the right book for you. The authors, Stanley and Danko interviewed the elite citizens of America, those with a net worth of more than one million dollars, and revealed their secrets for success.

Most of their findings resulted in a few rules like choosing your occupation wisely and living below your means. This book teaches about how to live a lifestyle that creates wealth and not how to invest heavily. As at 2017 November, the book had sold more than three million copies.

2. Rich dad poor dad

Rich dad poor dad is a successful book written by Robert Kiyosaki. In his book, Kiyosaki seeks to educate people on the level of financial literacy usually ignored by formal education.

Building wealth through investing in real estates, assets, financial independence, and intelligence as well as starting and owning businesses. The book was first published in 1997 and has sold over 32 million copies since then.

3. The intelligent investor

The intelligent investor is a book by Graham Benjamin and is based on value investing. If you are seeking to venture in stock market exchange then this is the best book for you. It teaches the investor not to regard the notions the prices quoted by the market when determining the value of the shares he owns.

The book also teaches the investor to concentrate more on the performances of his company rather than the irregular behavior of the market prices. The book has been helpful to many and as a result, has sold over this book has sold over a million copies since it was first published.

4. 48 laws of power

48 laws of power is one of the best-selling books in America. The author of the book is Robert Greene. He has incorporated the three thousand years of the history of power and came up with 48 crucial law that seeks to help people gain, observe and defend against the ultimate control. The book was first published in 1998 and has sold over 1.2 million copies since. It is most common with American prisons and elite business people.

Get to understand these 48 laws from the book and learn how to being control over your business.

5. Zero to one

Zero to one is a book by Peter Thiel. The book is about how to build a successful business. He talks of innovation as the only way to be successful. Thiel argues that the next billionaires will have to offer something different to the world. He has highlighted several other great ideas that would make you successful in business. This book is common worldwide and has sold more than 600,000 copies since it was published in 2014. It is an excellent book if you are a start-up entrepreneur.

6. Awaken the giant within

This is a book you have to read if you seek to find

the necessary techniques to take control of your life. The book is written by Tony Robbins and he insists on 3 essential things if you want to change your life:
-- You have to raise your standards and believe you can meet them.
-- What you do consistently is what changes your life
-- If you need to change your standards you have to change the perception about life and believe you can achieve the goals you have set.

This book is very popular among entrepreneurs and has sold over 2 million of its copies since it was first published in 1991.

7. The richest man in Babylon
If you need to be successful in business, this is the right type of book for you. The book talks of saving at least 10% of everything you earn and that you are not supposed to confuse your essential expenses with desires. The book emphasizes hard work which is essential in sharpening your skills and ensuring you have a reliable income stream. The book is written by George Samuel Clason and has sold over 2 million copies worldwide.

8. Grit

GRIT is a book by Angela Duckworth. Duckworth states in the book that successful people are mad by grit, a combination of perseverance and passion backed by talent. Talent is essential according to Duckworth. She explains that a combination of talent and GRIT builds skill which is essential in bringing about success.

She states further states that grit grows while talent is inborn. This is a book worth reading if you are keen on developing your skills in a bid to better your life. The book was first published in 2016 and is regarded as New York Times bestseller.

9. The 7 Habits of Highly Effective People

This is a self-help business book written by Stephen Covey. The book is based on an approach of being effective in attaining goals. Covey states that for one to be effective, they have to align themselves to the principles which he calls true north which is based on character ethics. He states that effectiveness is the balance of obtaining results while caring for that where the result was produced. The book was first published in 1989 and has sold more than 25 million copies since then.

10. Think and grow rich

Rich and grow rich is a book by Napoleon Hill and written in 1937. The book is based on increasing income and has several philosophies that can help you succeed in business or in your line or work. The book is one of the bestselling books in the world with over 100 million copies sold as at 2015.

Conclusion

If you need to be successful, then these are the kind of books you need to associate with. They have essentials as well as advises to being a success either in life, in education or in business. Grab any of these top 10 success books and change your life for the better.

THANK YOU VERY MUCH FOR READING THIS BOOK! I WISH YOU ALL THE BEST THINGS AND SUCCESS IN YOUR LIFE.

www.ingramcontent.com/pod-product-compliance
Lightning Source LLC
Chambersburg PA
CBHW031422210526
45464CB00005B/2002